FINGERPICKING COUNTRY

ISBN 978-0-634-09341-8

Visit Hal Leonard Online at www.halleonard.com

HAL•LEONARD®
CORPORATION

7777 W. BLUEMOUND RD. P.O. BOX 13819 MILWAUKEE, WI 53213

INTRODUCTION TO FINGERSTYLE GUITAR

Fingerstyle (a.k.a. fingerpicking) is a guitar technique that means you literally pick the strings with your right-hand fingers and thumb. This contrasts with the conventional technique of strumming and playing single notes with a pick (a.k.a. flatpicking). For fingerpicking, you can use any type of guitar: acoustic steel-string, nylon-string classical, or electric.

THE RIGHT HAND

The most common right-hand position is shown here.

Use a high wrist; arch your palm as if you were holding a ping-pong ball. Keep the thumb outside and away from the fingers, and let the fingers do the work rather than lifting your whole hand.

The thumb generally plucks the bottom strings with downstrokes on the left side of the thumb and thumbnail. The other fingers pluck the higher strings using upstrokes with the fleshy tip of the fingers and fingernails. The thumb and fingers should pluck one string per stroke and not brush over several strings.

Another picking option you may choose to use is called hybrid picking (a.k.a. plectrum-style fingerpicking). Here, the pick is usually held between the thumb and first finger, and the three remaining fingers are assigned to pluck the higher strings.

THE LEFT HAND

The left-hand fingers are numbered 1 through 4.

Be sure to keep your fingers arched, with each joint bent; if they flatten out across the strings, they will deaden the sound when you fingerpick. As a general rule, let the strings ring as long as possible when playing fingerstyle.

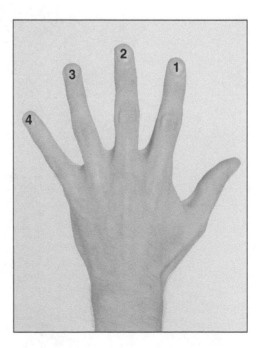

Always on My Mind

Words and Music by Wayne Thompson, Mark James and Johnny Christopher

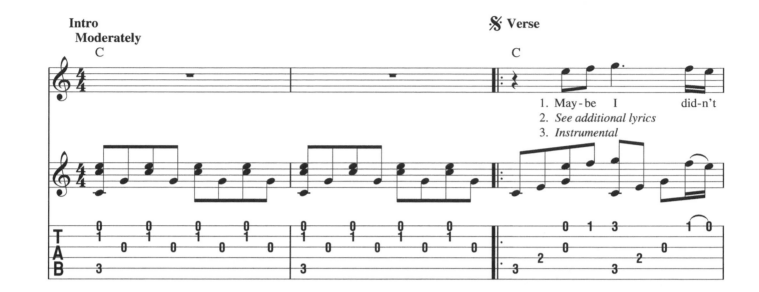

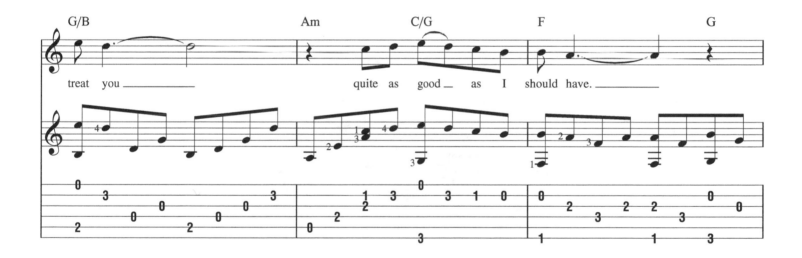

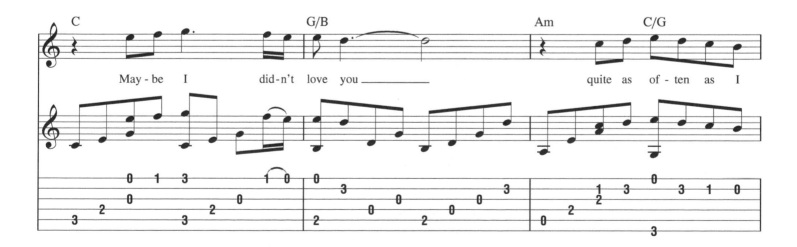

Additional Lyrics

2. Maybe I didn't hold you
   All those lonely, lonely times,
   And I guess I never told you
   I'm so happy that you're mine.
   If I made you feel second best,
   Girl, I'm so sorry, I was blind.

Blue Eyes Crying in the Rain

Words and Music by Fred Rose

Drop D tuning:
(low to high) D–A–D–G–B–E

1. In _____ the twi-light glow I see her, _ blue _____ eyes
2. *See additional lyrics*

cry-ing in the rain. When _____ we kissed good-bye and part - ed, _

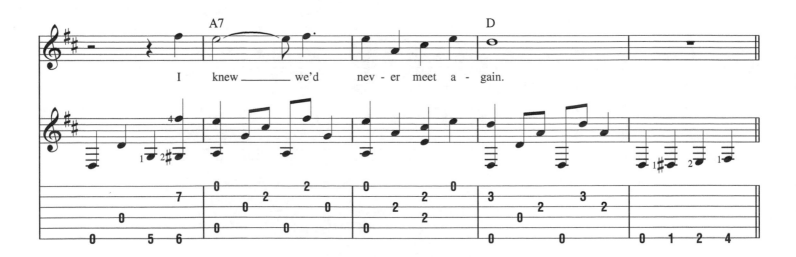

I knew _____ we'd nev - er meet a - gain.

Chorus

Love _____ is like a dy - ing em - ber, _____ on - ly mem - o - ries re -

See additional lyrics

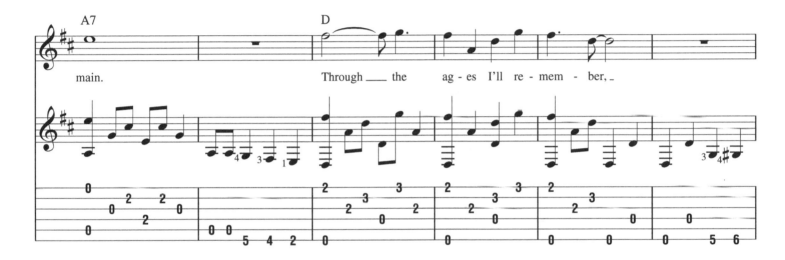

main. Through ____ the ag - es I'll re - mem - ber, _

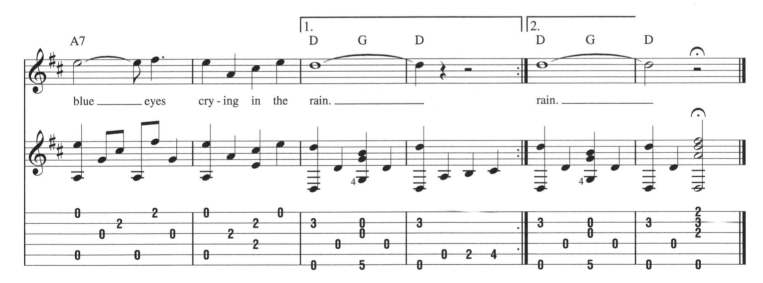

blue _____ eyes cry - ing in the rain. _____ rain.

Additional Lyrics

2. Now my hair has turned to silver.
   All my life I've loved in vain.
   I can see her star in heaven,
   Blue eyes crying in the rain.

Chorus Someday when we meet up yonder,
   We'll stroll hand in hand again
   In a land that knows no parting,
   Blue eyes crying in the rain.

By the Time I Get to Phoenix

Words and Music by Jimmy Webb

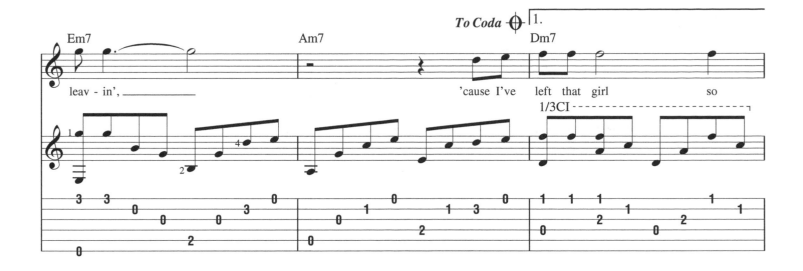

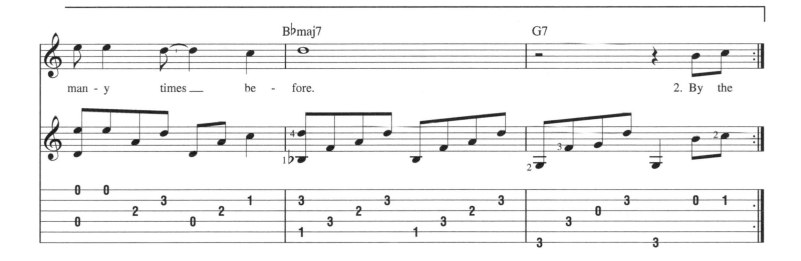

⊕ Coda

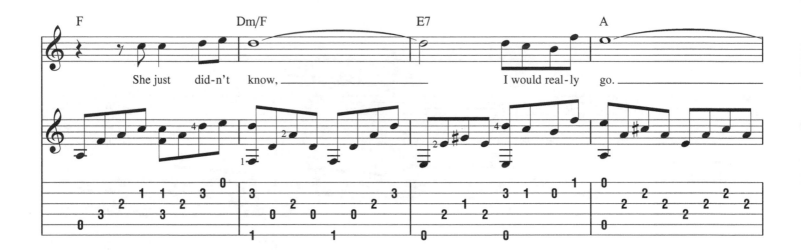

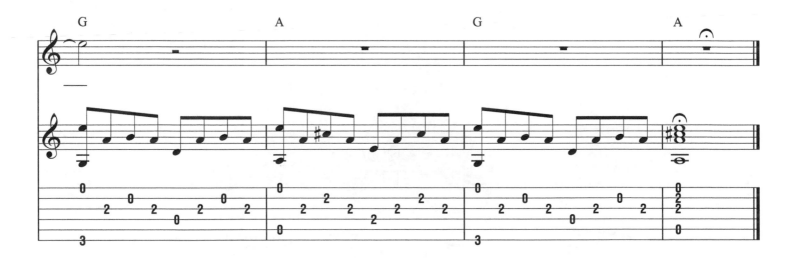

Additional Lyrics

2. By the time I make Albuquerque, she'll be workin'.
   She'll pro'bly stop at lunch and give me a call.
   But she'll just hear that phone keep on ringin'
   Off the wall, that's all.

3. By the time I make Oklahoma, she'll be sleepin'.
   She'll turn softly and call my name out low.
   And cry just to think I'd really leave her,
   Though time and time I've tried to tell her so.
   She just didn't know, I would really go.

Could I Have This Dance

from URBAN COWBOY

Words and Music by Wayland Holyfield and Bob House

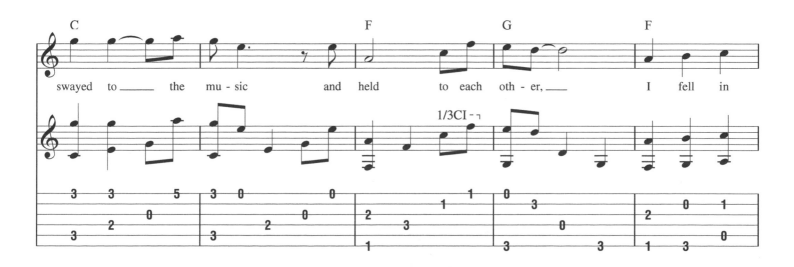

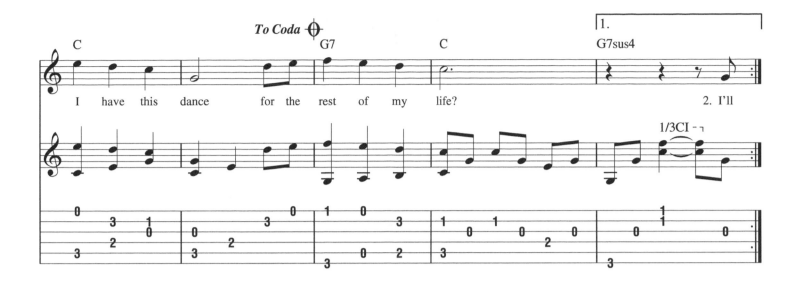

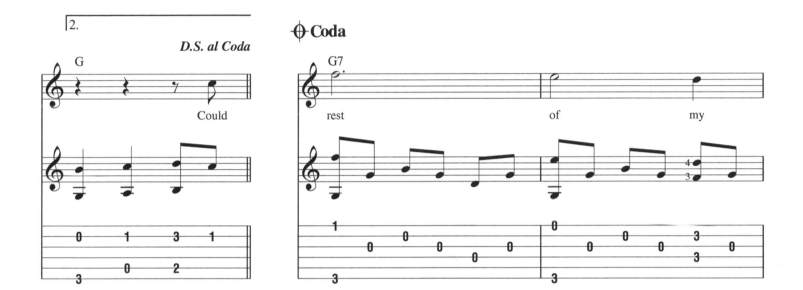

Additional Lyrics

2. I'll always remember that magic moment
   When I held you close to me.
   As we moved together, I knew forever
   You're all I'll ever need.

Crazy

Words and Music by Willie Nelson

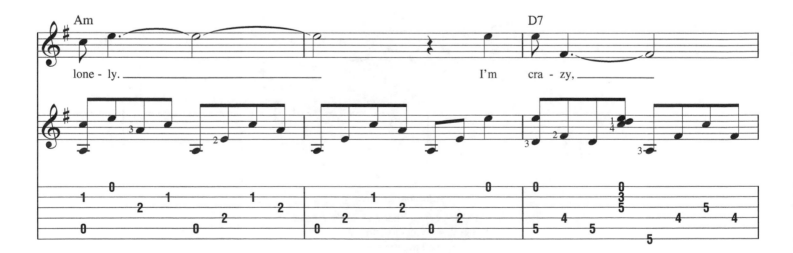

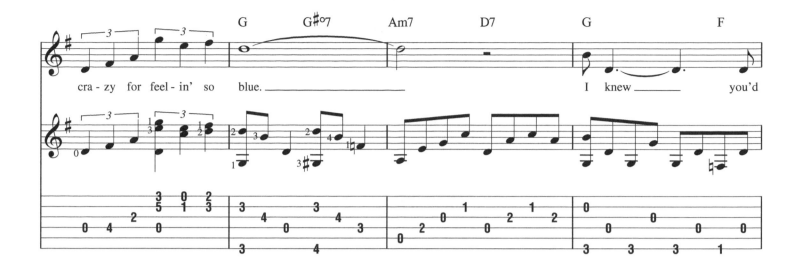

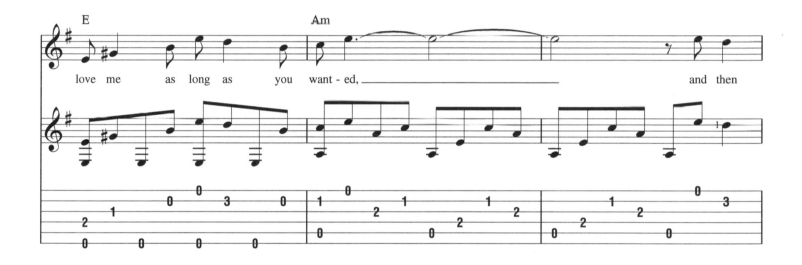

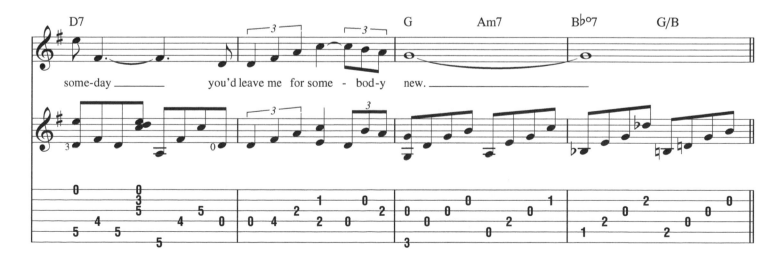

Wor - ry, _____ why do I let my - self wor - ry, _____

___ won - d'rin' _____ what in the world did I

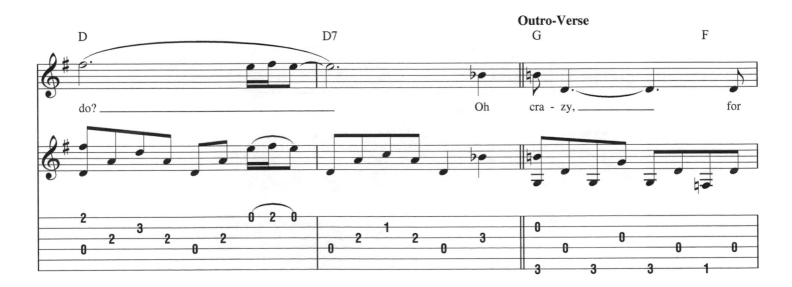

do? _____ Oh cra - zy, _____ for

Outro-Verse

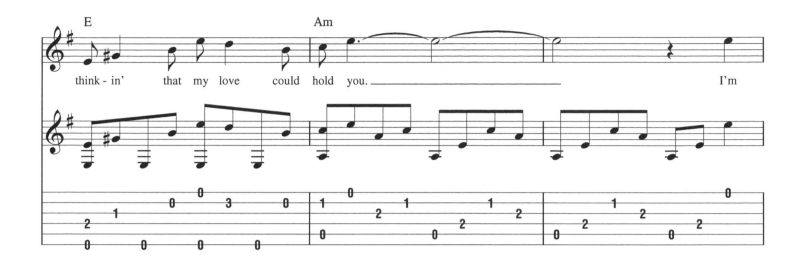

think - in' that my love could hold you. _____ I'm

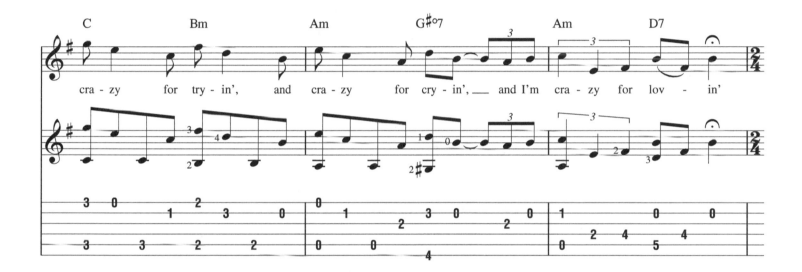

cra - zy for try - in', and cra - zy for cry - in', ___ and I'm cra - zy for lov - in'

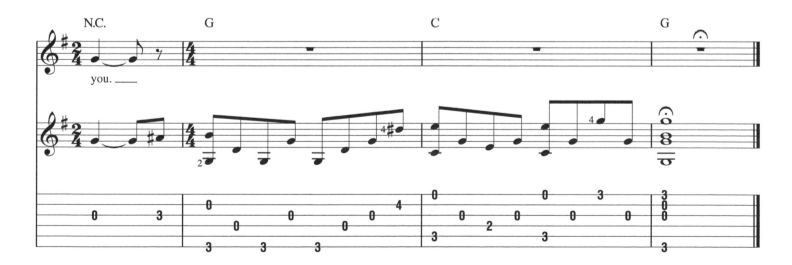

you. ___

Green Green Grass of Home

Words and Music by Curly Putman

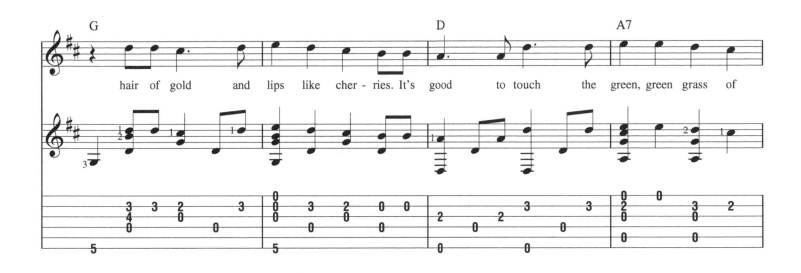

hair of gold and lips like cher - ries. It's good to touch the green, green grass of

Chorus

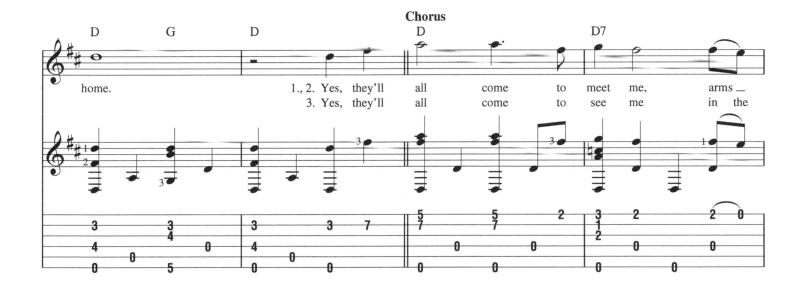

home. 1., 2. Yes, they'll all come to meet me, arms —
3. Yes, they'll all come to see me in the

1., 2.

reach - ing, smil - ing sweet - ly; it's good to touch the green, green grass of

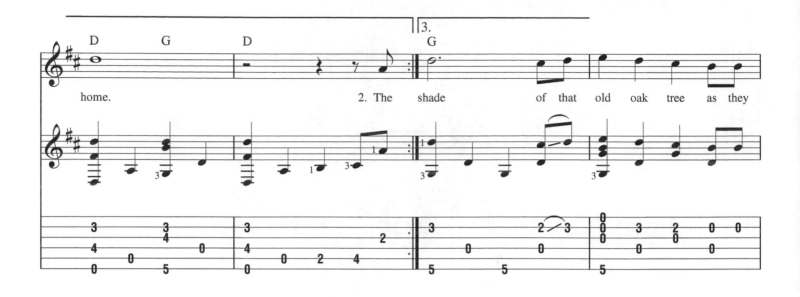

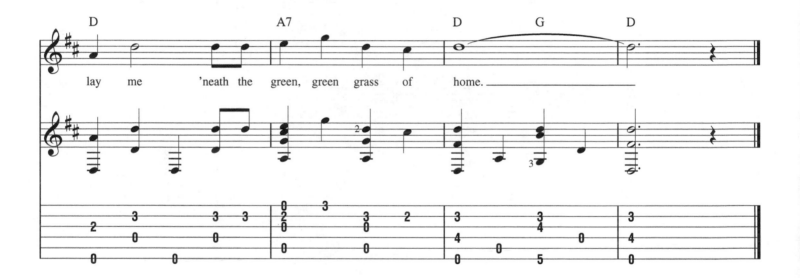

Additional Lyrics

2. The old house is still standing, though the paint is cracked and dry,
   And there's that old oak tree that I used to play on.
   Down the lane I walk with my sweet Mary,
   Hair of gold and lips like cherries.
   It's good to touch the green, green grass of home.

3. *Spoken:* *Then I awake and look around me at four gray walls that surround me,*
   And I realize that I was only dreaming.
   For there's a guard and there's a sad old padre.
   Arm in arm, we'll walk at daybreak,
   And again I'll touch the green, green grass of home.

He Stopped Loving Her Today

Words and Music by Bobby Braddock and Curly Putman

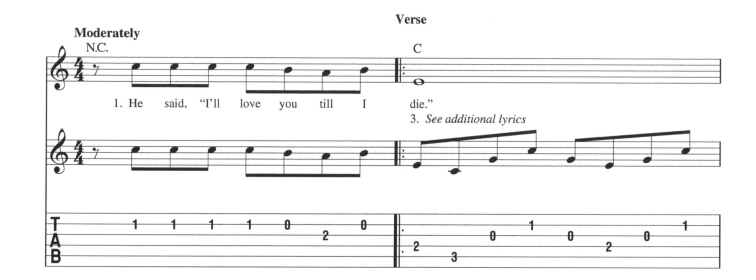

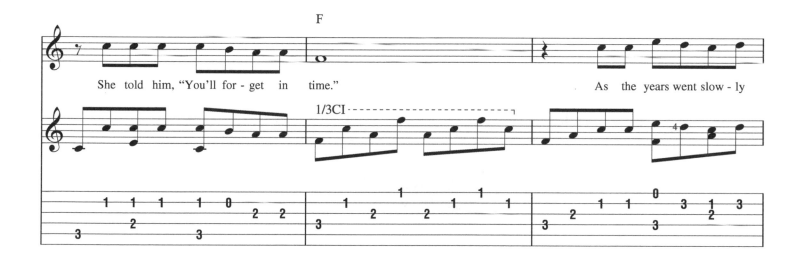

Chorus

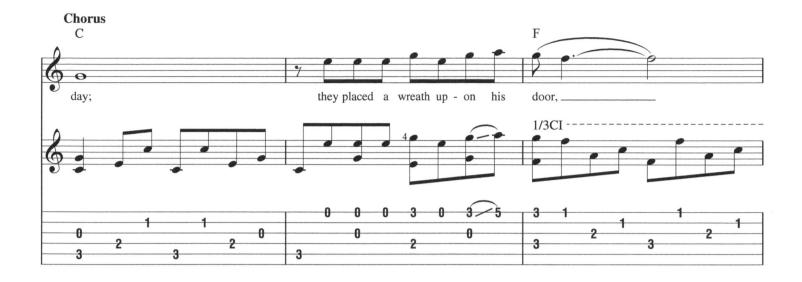

day;   they placed a wreath up - on his door, _____

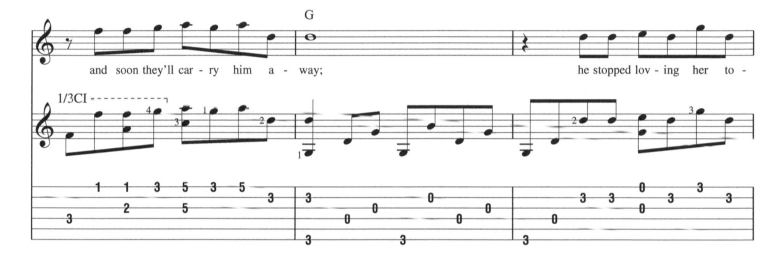

and soon they'll car - ry him a - way;   he stopped lov - ing her to -

To Coda ⊕   *D.S. al Coda*
(take 2nd ending)

⊕ **Coda**

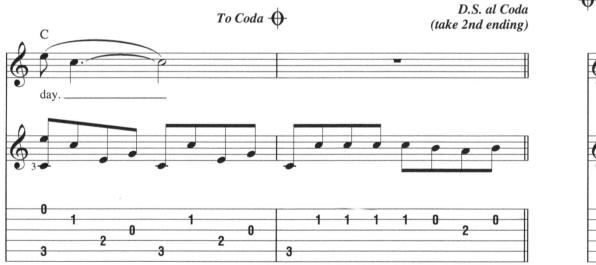

day. _____

Additional Lyrics

3. He kept some letters by his bed,
   Dated nineteen-sixty-two;
   He had underlined in red
   Ev'ry single "I love you."

4. I went to see him just today,
   Oh, but I didn't see no tears.
   All dressed up to go away;
   First time I'd seen him smile in years.

5. *Spoken: You know, she came to see him one last time;*
   We all wondered if she would,
   And it kept runing through my mind,
   This time he's over her for good.

Have I Told You Lately
That I Love You

Words and Music by Scott Wiseman

1. Have I told you late-ly that I love you? _____ Could I tell you
2., 3. *See additional lyrics*

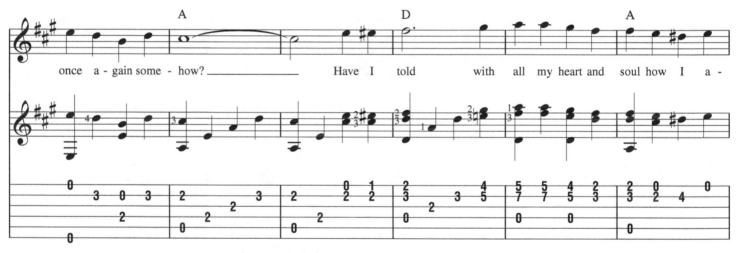

once a-gain some-how? _____ Have I told with all my heart and soul how I a-

dore you? Well, dar-ling, I'm tell-ing you now. _____ This heart would

Chorus

break in two if you re-fuse me. _____ I'm no good with-out you an-y-

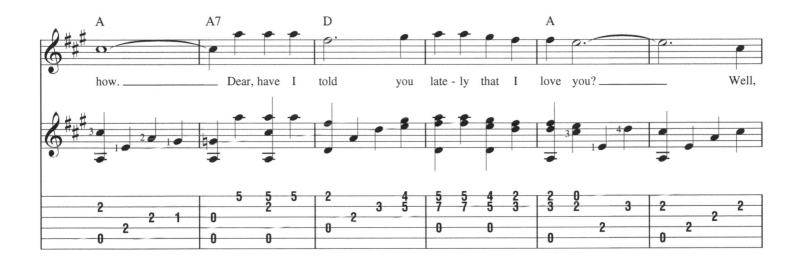

how. _____ Dear, have I told you late-ly that I love you? _____ Well,

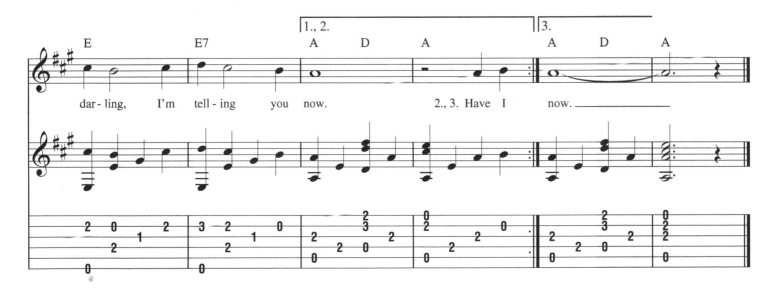

dar-ling, I'm tell-ing you now. 2., 3. Have I now. _____

Additional Lyrics

2. Have I told you lately that I love you
   When the stars are shining in the sky?
   Have I told you why the nights are long when you're not with me?
   Well, darling, I'm telling you now.

3. Have I told you lately when I'm sleeping
   Ev'ry dream is you somehow?
   Have I told you I'd like to share my love forever?
   Well, darling, I'm telling you now.

He'll Have to Go

Words and Music by Joe Allison and Audrey Allison

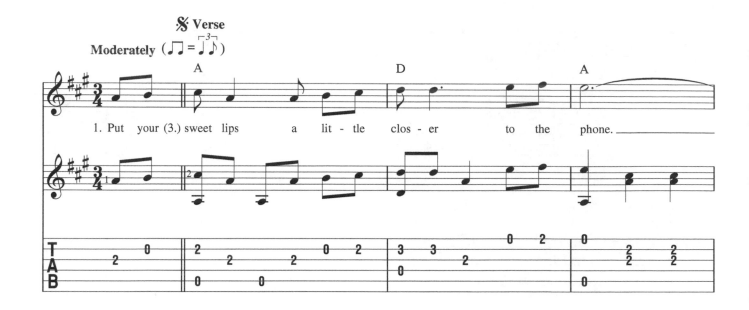

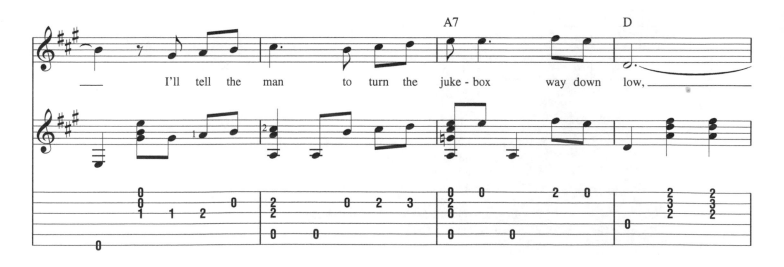

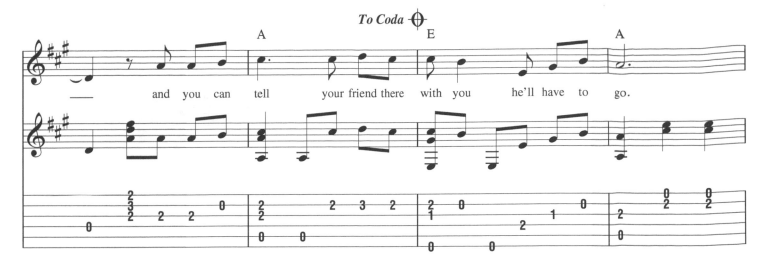

and you can tell   your friend there   with you   he'll have to   go.

Verse

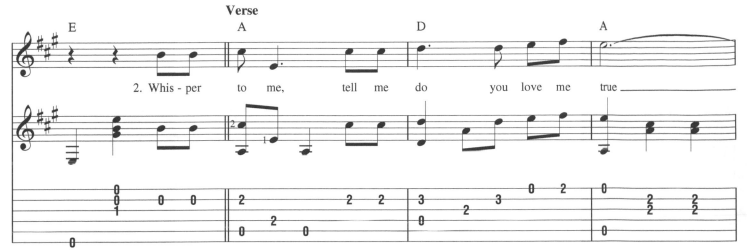

2. Whis - per   to   me,   tell   me   do   you   love   me   true

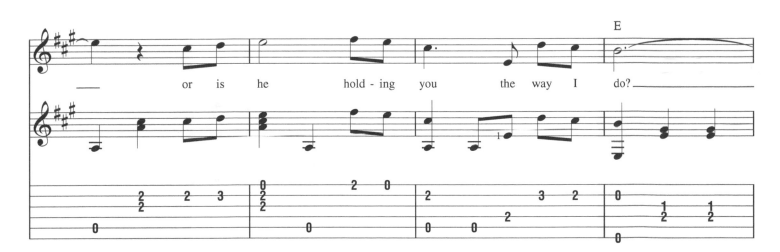

or   is   he   hold - ing   you   the   way   I   do?

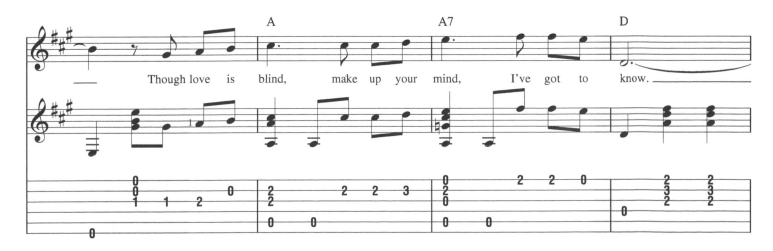

Though love   is   blind,   make   up   your   mind,   I've   got   to   know.

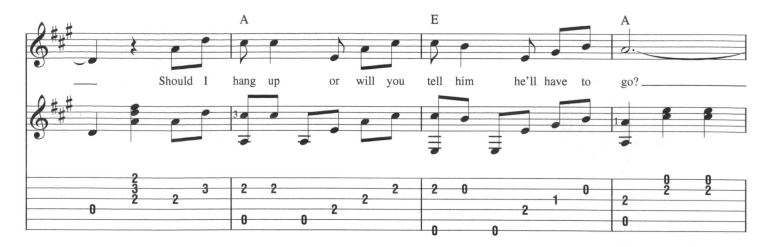

Should I hang up or will you tell him he'll have to go? ____

Bridge

____ You can't say the words I want to hear while you're with an - oth - er

man. Do you want me, an - swer "Yes" or "No", dar - ling, I will un - der -

D.S. al Coda

stand. 3. Put your

⊕ Coda

Slowly

with you he'll have to go. ____

28

King of the Road

Words and Music by Roger Miller

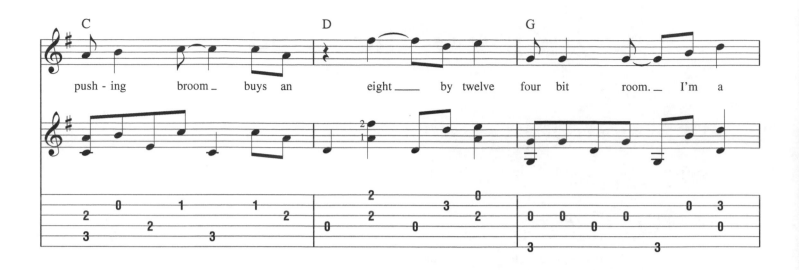

push - ing broom _ buys an eight ____ by twelve four bit room. _ I'm a

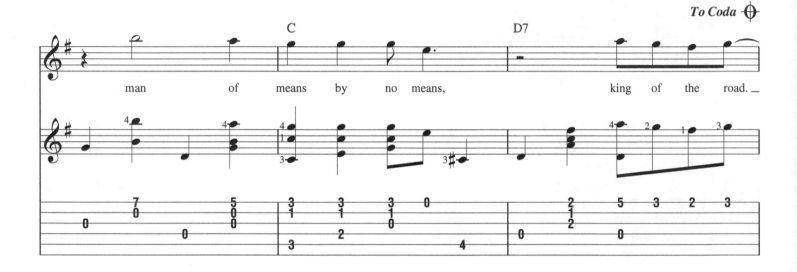

To Coda ⊕

man _ of means by no means, king of the road. _

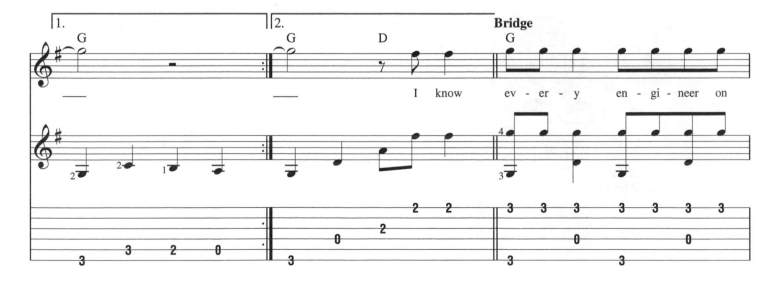

1. 2. **Bridge**

_ _ I know ev - er - y en - gi - neer on

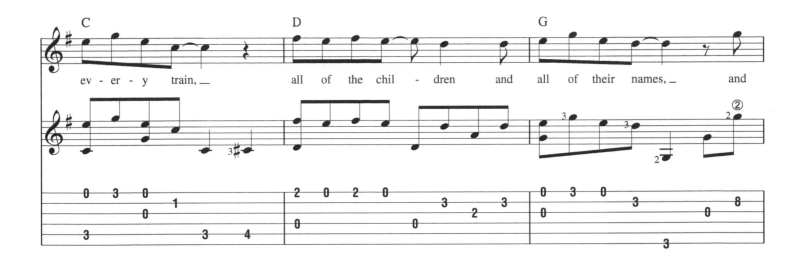

ev - er - y train, _____ all of the chil - dren and all of their names, _____ and

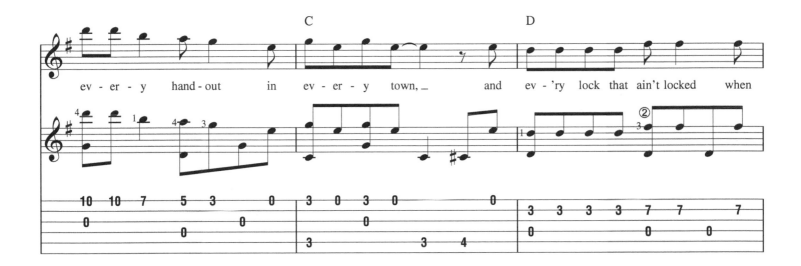

ev - er - y hand - out in ev - er - y town, _____ and ev - 'ry lock that ain't locked when

D.C. al Coda 𝄌 **Coda**

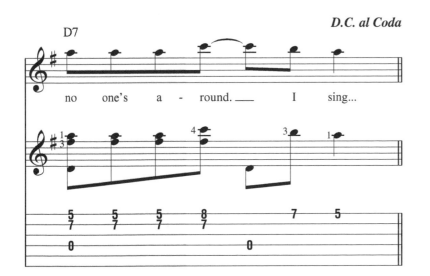

no one's a - round. _____ I sing...

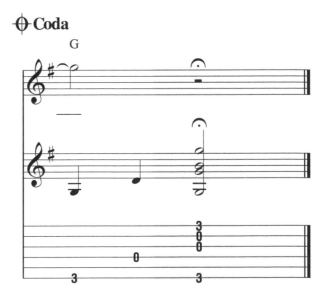

Additional Lyrics

2. Third box car, midnight train, destination: Bangor, Maine.
   Old worn out suit and shoes; I don't pay no union dues.
   I smoke old stogies I have found, short, but not too big around.
   I'm a man of means by no means, king of the road.

31

I Walk the Line

Words and Music by John R. Cash

Intro
Moderately

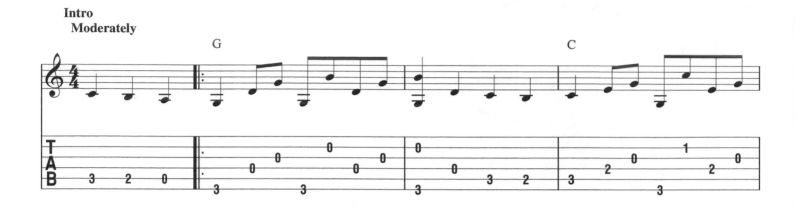

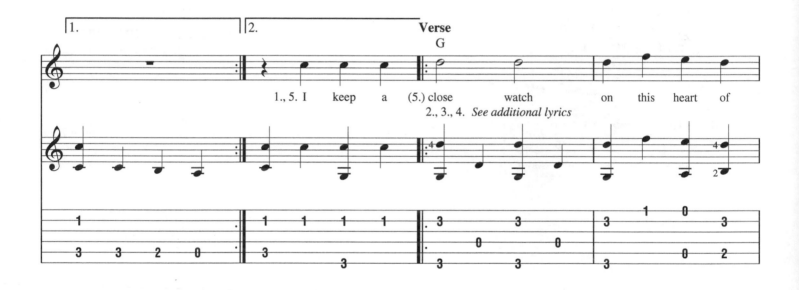

1., 5. I keep a (5.) close watch on this heart of
2., 3., 4. *See additional lyrics*

mine. _____ I keep my eyes wide o - pen all the

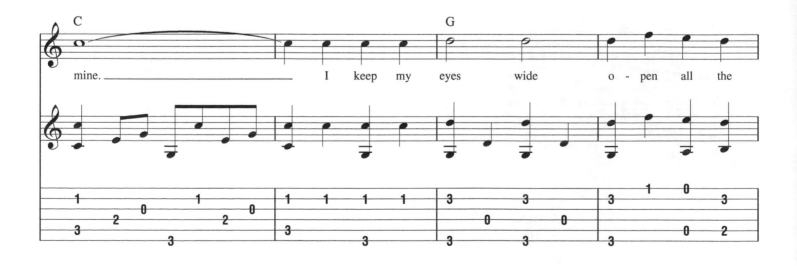

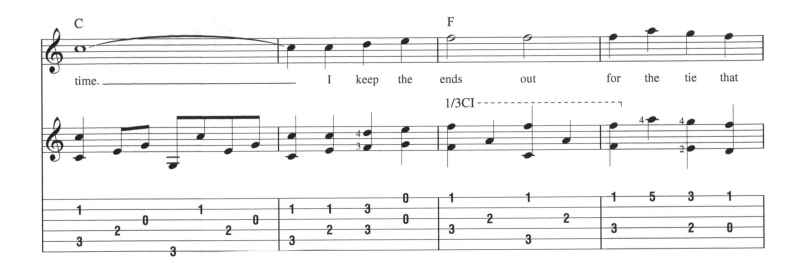

Additional Lyrics

2. I find it very, very easy to be true.
   I find myself alone when each day is through.
   Yes, I'll admit that I'm a fool for you.
   Because you're mine, I walk the line.

3. As sure as night is dark and day is light,
   I keep you on my mind both day and night.
   And happiness I've known proves that it's right.
   Because you're mine, I walk the line.

4. You've got a way to keep me on your side.
   You give me cause for love that I can't hide.
   For you I know I'd even try to turn the tide.
   Because you're mine, I walk the line.

I'm So Lonesome I Could Cry

Words and Music by Hank Williams

whin - ing low. I'm so lone - some I could ___

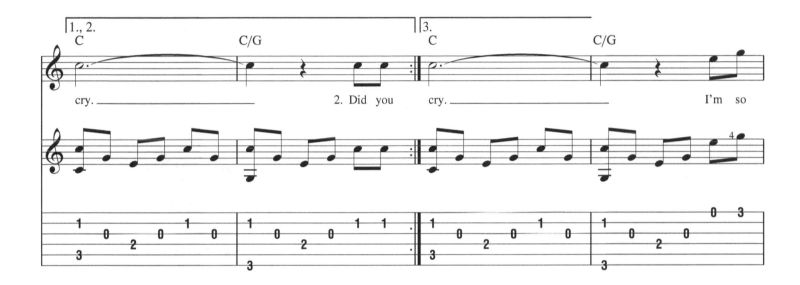

1., 2.
cry. ___

2. Did you cry. ___

3.
I'm so

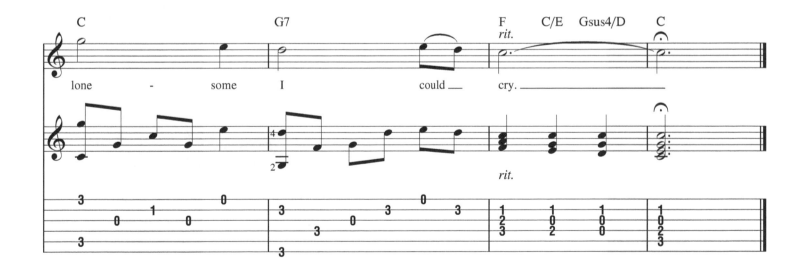

lone - some I could ___ cry. ___

rit.

Additional Lyrics

2. Did you ever see a robin weep
   When leaves begin to die?
   Like me he's lost the will to live.
   I'm so lonesome I could cry.

3. The silence of a falling star
   Lights up a purple sky.
   And as I wonder where you are
   I'm so lonesome I could cry.
   I'm so lonesome I could cry.

Make the World Go Away

Words and Music by Hank Cochran

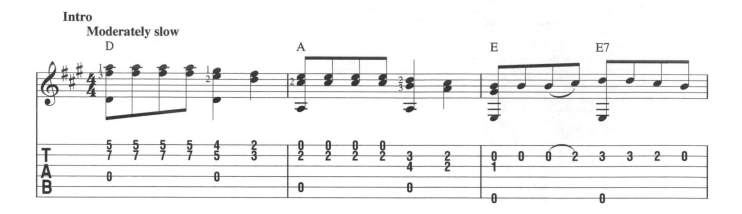

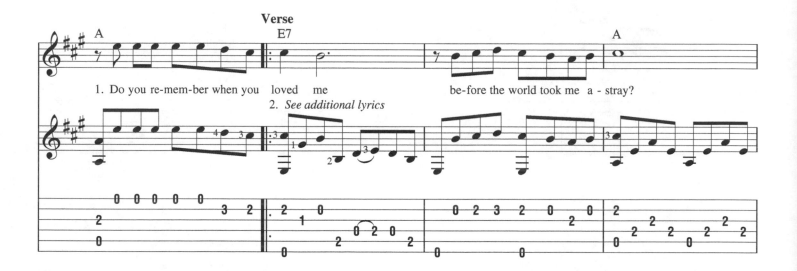

1. Do you re-mem-ber when you loved me be-fore the world took me a - stray?
2. *See additional lyrics*

If you do, then for - give me, and make the world go a - way.

Chorus

Make the world go a - way, and get it off _ my _ shoul - ders.

Say the things you used to say, and make the world _ go a -

way. 2. I'm sor - ry if I way.

Additional Lyrics

2. I'm sorry if I hurt you,
   I'll make it up day by day.
   Just say you love me like you used to,
   And make the world go away.

Oh, Lonesome Me

Words and Music by Don Gibson

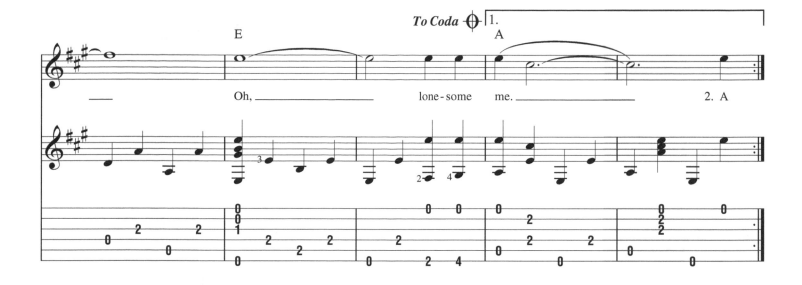

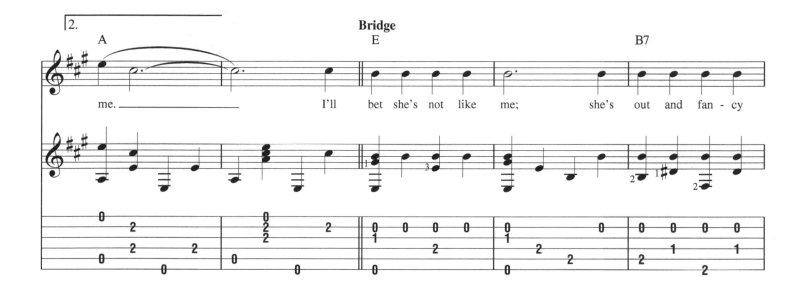

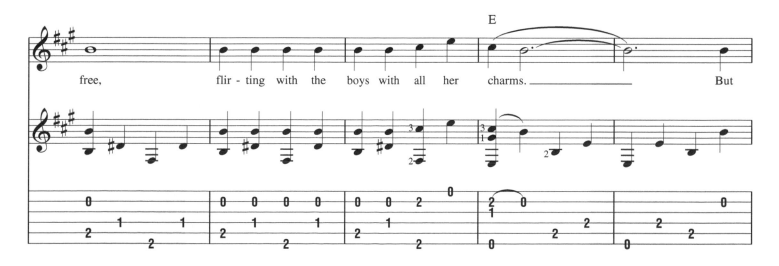

B7

I still love her so   and, broth-er, don't you know   I'd   wel-come her right

D.S. al Coda

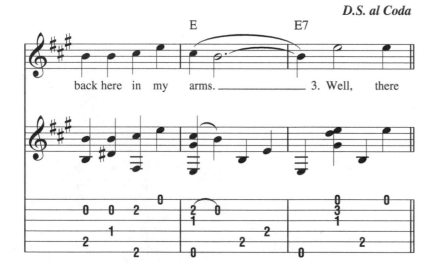

E   E7

back here in my arms. _____ 3. Well,   there

⊕ **Coda**

A

me. _____

Outro

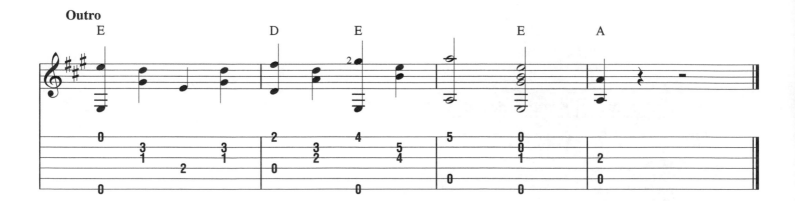

E   D   E   E   A

Additional Lyrics

2. A bad mistake I'm making by just hangin' 'round,
   I know that I should have some fun and paint the town.
   A lovesick fool that's blind and just can't see.
   Oh, lonesome me.

3. Well, there must be some way I can lose these lonesome blues.
   Forget about the past and find somebody new.
   I've thought of everything from A to Z.
   Oh, lonesome me.

You Are My Sunshine

Words and Music by Jimmie Davis and Charles Mitchell

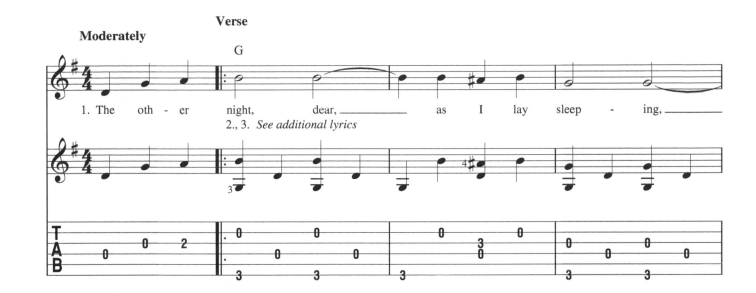

1. The oth-er night, dear, _____ as I lay sleep - ing, _____
2., 3. *See additional lyrics*

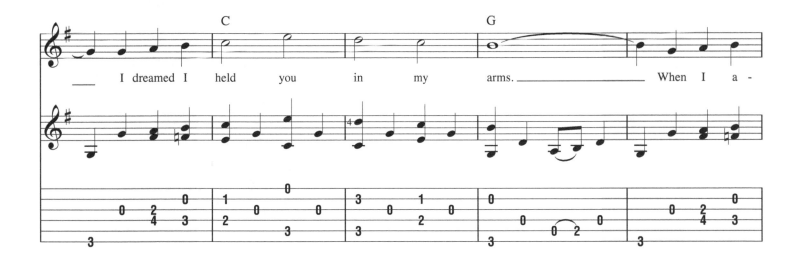

_____ I dreamed I held you in my arms. _____ When I a -

woke, dear, _____ I was mis - tak - en _____ and I

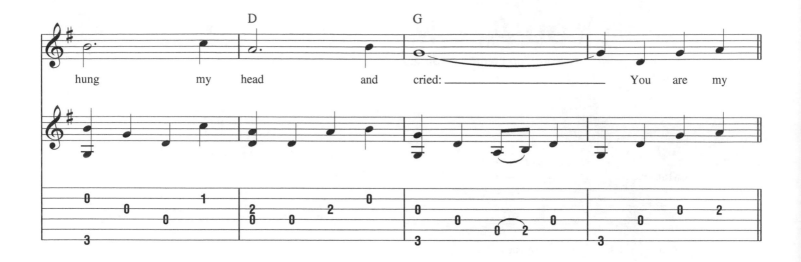

hung   my   head   and   cried: _____ You   are   my

Chorus

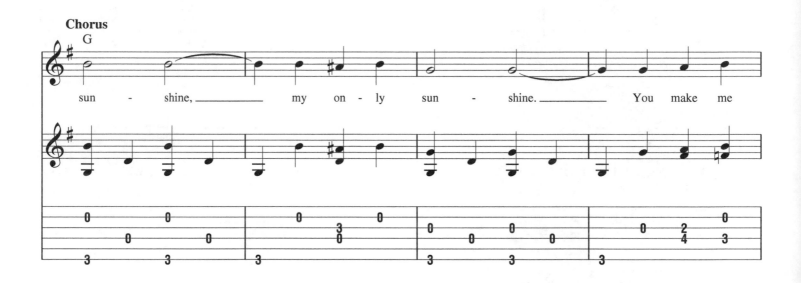

sun - shine, _____ my on - ly sun - shine. _____ You make me

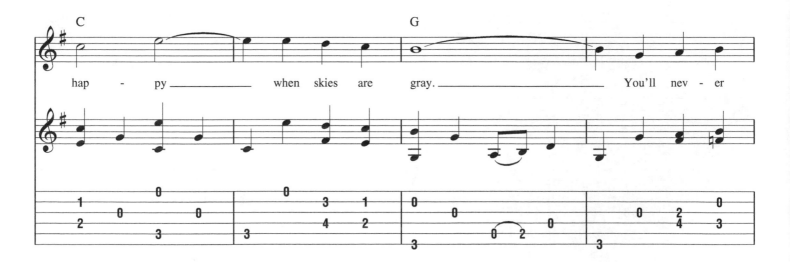

hap - py _____ when skies are gray. _____ You'll nev - er

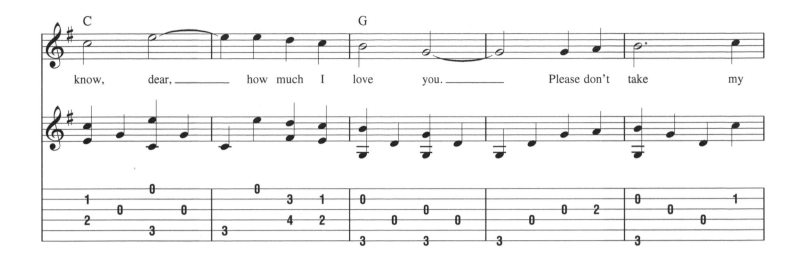

know,   dear, _____ how much I love   you. _____   Please don't take   my

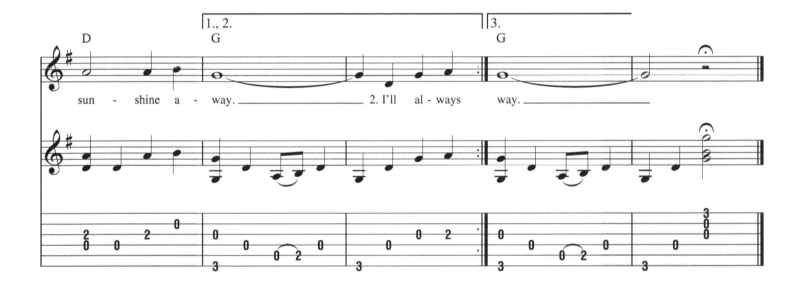

sun - shine a - way. _____ 2. I'll al - ways   way. _____

Additional Lyrics

2. I'll always love you and make you happy
   If you will only say the same.
   But if you leave me to love another,
   You'll regret it all some day.

3. You told me once, dear, you really loved me
   And no one else could come between.
   But now you've left me and love another;
   You have shattered all my dreams.

Tennessee Waltz

Words and Music by Redd Stewart and Pee Wee King

me. I re - mem - ber the night and the Ten - nes - see

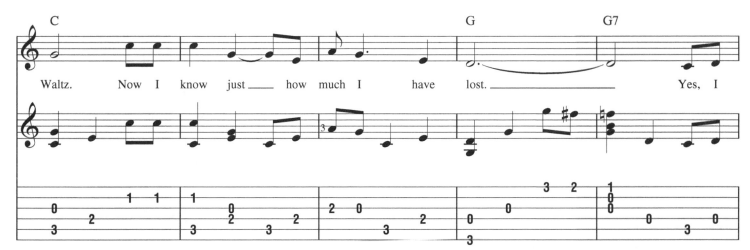

Waltz. Now I know just how much I have lost. Yes, I

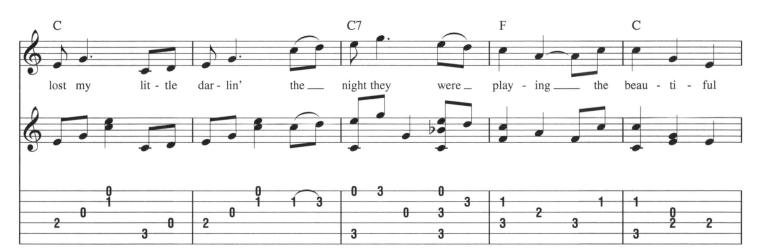

lost my lit - tle dar - lin' the night they were play - ing the beau - ti - ful

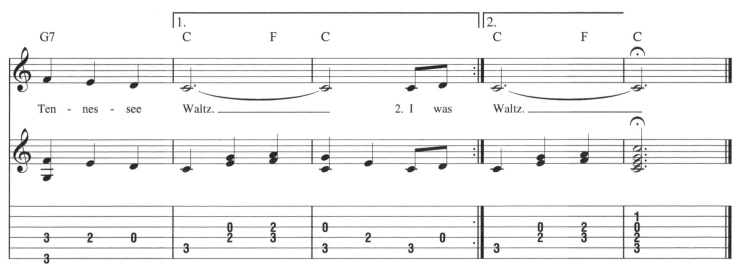

Ten - nes - see Waltz. 2. I was Waltz.

Your Cheatin' Heart

Words and Music by Hank Williams

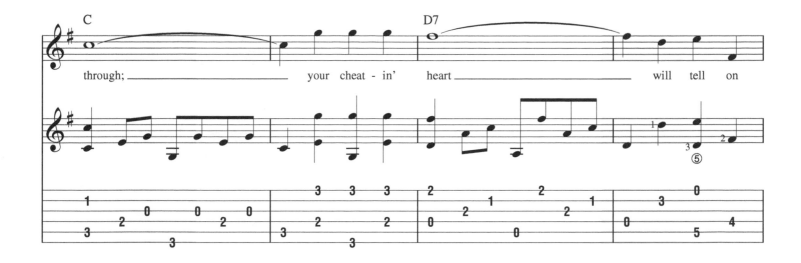

through; _____ your cheat - in' heart _____ will tell on

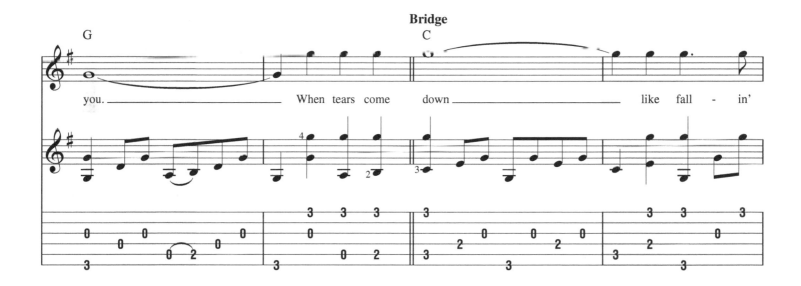

you. _____ When tears come down _____ like fall - in'

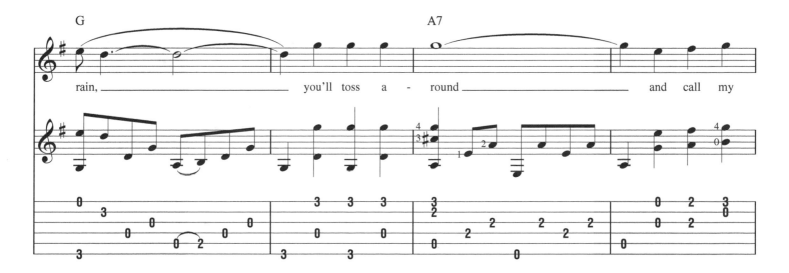

rain, _____ you'll toss a - round _____ and call my

Outro-Verse

name. ____ You'll walk the __ floor ____ the way I

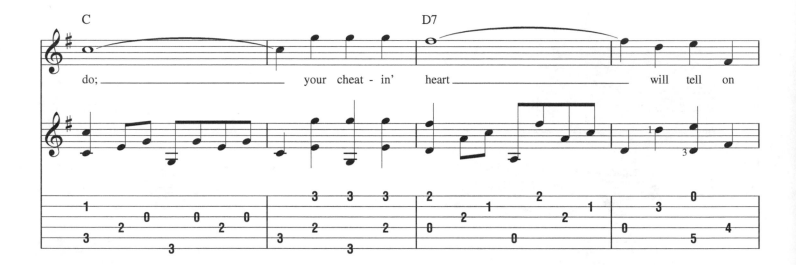

do; ____ your cheat - in' heart ____ will tell on

you. ____ 2. Your cheat - in' __ you. ____

Additional Lyrics

2. Your cheatin' heart will pine someday
And crave the love you threw away.
The time will come when you'll be blue;
Your cheatin' heart will tell on you.